How to Ace Your Phone Interview

© Copyright Peggy McKee, 2018

About the Author

Peggy McKee is an expert resource and a dedicated advocate for job seekers. As the CEO of Career Confidential, her years of experience as a nationally-known recruiter for sales and marketing jobs give her a unique perspective and advantage in developing the tools and strategies that help job seekers stand head and shoulders above the competition.

Peggy has been named **#1** on the list of the <u>Top 25 Most Influential Online Recruiters by HR Examiner</u>, and has been quoted in articles from <u>CNN</u>, <u>CAP TODAY</u>, <u>Yahoo!HotJobs</u>, and more. She is the official <u>SelfGrowth.com Expert Guide to Interviewing Skills</u>.

Originally from Oklahoma, Peggy grew up on a 1000-acre ranch. She earned a B.S. in Chemistry and an M.B.A. in Marketing from the University of Oklahoma, and went on to great achievements in the medical sales arena.

In 1999 Peggy founded PHC Consulting, a medical sales recruiting firm. When she consistently found herself offering advice to jobseekers who weren't her candidates, she developed a new business model to offer personalized career coaching as well as the tools to help you thrive and succeed in the job search...and Career Confidential was born.

Today, Career Confidential offers more than 30 products, tools, and webinars for job seekers. Peggy receives positive responses every day from candidates who have used Career Confidential tools to land the job of their dreams, and she loves that she has been able to contribute to their success.

Peggy lives in Texas with her husband and two children and loves ranch work, trail riding, and her favorite horse, Lucky.

Letter from the Author

Phone interviews...as a recruiter (14 years), I call these phone *screens*. Why? Because, when I call a candidate on the phone to ask those first few questions, I'm looking to make a decision: Yes or no, good or bad, move forward or stop right here.

In a phone screen, moving to the next step should be your goal but most folks don't take this very important career conversation seriously enough. For anything to be a great experience, we have to plan, prepare and execute. Then, of course, there is the follow up!

I applaud you for reading this book, because you're taking more action than most. In order to get the job offers you want and go to the places you want in your career and life, you need to do more, and be better than others. This book will help you achieve that.

Enjoy this book filled with my best phone interview tips from 14 years of conversations with thousands of candidates. Read it carefully, and use it to prepare for your next phone interview.

Best of luck (the harder you work, the luckier you get),

Peggy McKee
Career and Interview Coach
CEO Career Confidential
https://CareerConfidential.com

> *"All our dreams can come true,*
> *if we have the courage to pursue them."*
> *–Walt Disney*

Table of Contents

Phone Interview Tips - #1

Understand the Importance of This Call

How Important Telephone Interviews Really Are

A phone interview is never "just" a phone interview. It's the first step in the hiring process. You will never get to the second step (the face-to-face interview) if you don't do a great job here.

Phone interviews are the gating process companies use to whittle down their list of candidates. That's why they are also called phone screens. Companies use these quick, inexpensive interviews to look for reasons to weed you out. You will not get a second chance.

This is the make-it-or-break-it moment that decides whether or not you can be in the running for the job.

Why Companies Do Phone Interviews

Hiring managers (that's the person who would be your boss) don't have time to face-to-face interview all the people applying for the position. So they run you through this conversational test to see if you're worth spending an hour with in a regular interview. This way, they can meet with more people in less time.

They get some bonuses out of it, too. In a phone interview, it's much easier for them to cut the call short because they've decided against you in the first few minutes. No commitment, no expense, no muss, no fuss.

Why People Succeed or Fail in Phone Interviews

Job seekers fail in the phone interview for two major reasons:

(1) they don't take it seriously enough, and
(2) they don't successfully meet its unique challenges.

All interviews are really about communication, which can be difficult enough. However, the vast majority of communication between two people is visual. In a phone interview, neither of you can see all of the micro-expressions and gestures that give your words clarity and convey meaning. So you are at a disadvantage.

However...if you take the phone interview as seriously as a face-to-face interview, and you learn to work with the unique circumstances of a phone interview, you can easily succeed.

Why This Book?

Each tip in this book will give you another "lesson" in phone interviews that will make sure you succeed in your goal, which is to get invited to interview in person. You'll discover how to prepare, what to say, how to follow up, and much more.

Phone Interview Tips - #2

Check Your Voicemail Greeting, Ring backs, and Message-Takers

This is really a *pre*-phone interview tip. Often, the company or recruiter will call you to set up the phone interview (and sometimes, they'll call a few minutes early for a scheduled interview in order to catch you off guard and see how you react). If you can't answer the phone, their first impression of you is whatever is on your recorded greeting—or whoever answers your phone.

For a professional, friendly greeting:

- Keep your message to 30 seconds or less (no music)
- Eliminate any background noise
- Possibly offer an alternative way to contact you, such as your email address

What is the best voicemail message? Short and sweet:

"Hi, this is Joe Smith. Please leave a message and I'll get back to you as soon as possible."

"You've reached the Burtons. Please leave a message."

"You've reached 555-555-1212. Please leave a message." (If you are not comfortable leaving your name.)

A very nice touch is to show some enthusiasm and thank the person for calling:

"Hi, this is Jane Smith. I appreciate your call, but I am not available right now. Please leave a message and I will call you back soon."

After you get the job, you can change your voicemail back to anything you want.

Worst Voicemail Greetings I've Ever Heard

- The one that made me listen to the person's favorite song before I could leave my message (it wasn't MY favorite song)

- The one that was recorded by charming (I'm sure) but difficult-to-understand 3-year-old

- The one that tried to be funny but wasn't: "How do you leave an idiot in suspense? Leave a message and I'll get back to you." (...leaves you feeling all warm and fuzzy, doesn't it?)

Ring back Tones

If you have changed the standard ringing sound that callers hear to your favorite song or some other custom sound, change it back—at least while you're in the job search.

Message-Takers

If roommates or family members will be answering your phone, either train them to answer it professionally (which means being ready to take a message complete with name and telephone number—and making sure that you actually get the message), or insist that no one answer the phone and instead let it go to your very professional voicemail greeting.

If your cell is your primary number...

Be cognizant of where you are and what you're doing when you answer the phone. If you're going to answer the call of a recruiter or hiring manager, don't be in a very noisy store or out of breath from running. If you're not already in a quiet spot, it is better to let it go to voicemail so you can get to somewhere appropriate to call back.

*"You never get a second chance to make
a good first impression."*
- Will Rogers

Control the Time of Your Call

You have the power to control the day and time of your phone interview—and it is in your best interests to use it. Why?

1) You need enough time to prepare. This phone interview is a very big deal. If you blow it here, you don't get another chance, so you want enough time to prepare and research for this interview very well.

2) You'll have a better interview because you're always going to come across stronger and more effectively if you schedule the interview for a time when you're calm, alert, and focused.

   (Personally, I would never, ever schedule a phone interview first thing in the morning. I need a little while to warm up first. On the other hand, I have a friend who is at her most chipper in the wee hours. So for her, earlier is better.)

3) You can leave yourself a time cushion in case the interview goes longer than expected (a great sign!). I've seen phone interviews go over the allotted time by 5, 10, or even 30 minutes. (If they don't tell you how long they expect the call to take, ask.)

Setting a time for a phone interview is just like setting any other appointment. It shows good time management. Most hiring managers won't have a problem with it at all, and in fact expect to schedule the interview with you.

There's always an exception to the rule, of course...so what happens if they call you out of the blue and want to talk about the job right then? You can choose not to answer it and let it go to your voicemail (but return the call as soon as possible). If you do answer it, it is perfectly acceptable to say, "I'm so glad you called. I would love to talk to you now, but I'm really not going to be able to give this the attention it deserves right at this moment. Can we talk tomorrow morning?" (Or whenever a good time for you is.)

"The definition of insanity is doing the same thing over and over and expecting different results."
–Benjamin Franklin

A Tip for Scheduling Phone Interviews
If You Are Employed

Please do not schedule your phone interviews during your normal work time—unless you have taken time off.

If the interviewer realizes you are using company time to conduct your job search, they will question your ethics and might decide not to move forward with you on that basis alone.

*I am curious....Do you ask outright
in your phone interviews if they will move you
forward to the face-to-face?*

*Let me know if you do or don't in your
comments on the book.
(We'll be talking about this later—Tip #35.)*

Control the Location of Your Call

Bad locations for any phone interview:

- Restaurants or coffee houses (too noisy and unpredictable)
- Bookstores or libraries (you'll be the one who's too noisy)
- Parks (nature can be loud)
- Your current office (too risky)
- Your car (especially if you're driving!)

The only good spot for any phone interview: **your home.**

At home, you have control over your environment and can keep it quiet. That being said, you have to exercise that control—which means no pets, no kids, and no significant others, either.

Make sure that all creatures big and small in your house are occupied elsewhere, and that the two-legged varieties (big and small) understand that if they interrupt you, there had better be gushing blood involved.

An emergency involving an ambulance is the only truly acceptable reason for your call to be interrupted.

What do you do if something interrupts your call?

No matter how hard you try, things of the non-emergency variety still sometimes happen. The dog barks. FedEx shows up at the door. You can get interrupted for a lot of reasons. Hiring managers understand that, but at the same time, they will be looking to see how you deal with the unexpected. What do you do?

First, keep your cool. If the distraction isn't going away, say, "Excuse me, please," deal with the issue, apologize for the interruption, and steer the conversation back to where you were in the interview.

Maintain your professionalism and your control. If you do, you will provide that hiring manager with a very clear picture of how you deal with interruptions or difficult situations on the job, which can be very impressive.

Use the Phone That Never Fails

The best phone for your interview is always a good old- fashioned land-line. (A cordless phone works, as long as you are *certain* it's charged.) Why a landline? The sound quality is better, there's no risk of dropping the call, and you never have to ask, "Can you hear me now?"

If you don't have a landline, and will use a cell phone no matter what I tell you, follow these **cell phone rules**:

1) Make sure your cell phone has a good signal. Call a friend before your interview starts to make sure all the signals are connecting like they're supposed to. Bad reception will ruin your call.

2) Make sure your phone is charged. You can prepare to an extreme degree, with every single detail taken care of...but if your phone dies during the call, the interviewer will think you are unorganized, unprepared, and not worth talking to again.

Phone Interview Tips - #6

Know Who You're Interviewing with—
HR or the Hiring Manager?

In a larger company, your first phone interview is likely to be with Human Resources, rather than the actual hiring manager (the person who will be your boss). In a smaller company, you might speak with the actual hiring manager first. However, usually doesn't mean always, so be sure to ask.

When the interview is scheduled (through email or a phone call), ask who you'll be interviewing with. They will usually tell you "Jane Smith, from HR" or "Sue Jones, the Accounting Director". If they just give you a name and you don't recognize it, ask for clarification: "And this person is...?" You want name and title.

Why should you care about knowing the difference? HR and Hiring Managers are coming to this interview from different places, so they are looking for different things. (Plus, HR interviews tend to be shorter than hiring manager ones, so you can plan accordingly.)

HR's function in the hiring process is to be a gatekeeper. Their job is to present qualified candidates with no red flags for the hiring manager to choose from. So their focus is "Do you have the basic qualifications and is there anything wrong with you?" They are (more than anyone else) looking for someone safe that won't make them look bad if they present you to the hiring manager. Be aware that you are playing defense here.

Hiring managers are looking less critically at your potential problems, and more intensely at your fit for the job: What have you done? What can you do? What can you bring to the team? Do you have the potential for fitting into the company well, and can they get along with you? In this interview, you're switching from defense to offense. Tell them why you would be an asset to them.

Remember that the job search is a sales process and you have to communicate in the language of your customer. Tell them what matters to THEM as they consider you for this job.

Hint... Ask How Much Time to Allow For This Call

When they schedule your call, ask how much time they think it will take. If they tell you 10-15 minutes, it's probably a simple screening call with HR. If they tell you more than 30 minutes, you'll probably be speaking in greater depth with the actual hiring manager.

"You were born to win, but to be a winner, you must plan to win, prepare to win, and expect to win."
–Zig Ziglar

Phone Interview Tips - #7

Research the Company

"What do you know about our company?"

This is a reasonable question you are likely to be asked. Hit a home run with your answer by doing your research on the company.

- Start with the **corporate website** to see what the company does and how large it is. See how technologically-savvy they are based on how well the website is done. You'll get a sense of corporate values from their mission statement.

- Then go to **Google** for news about the company. Are they growing? Have they started any projects? Have they been hit with lawsuits? What are others saying about this company?

- Check them out on **LinkedIn**. Corporate pages on LinkedIn give you additional information you can't get from the website.

  ** Also, check out the profiles of **employees** who work at the company. What's their background? How long have they been there? Those are big clues for you.

- Look at the company's **Facebook** page, if they have one, for less formal information. It gives you a different perspective.

- Find them on **Twitter**. You might or might not be able to find company tweets. But you might easily find employee tweets, which can be pretty valuable for you.

- Ask your **network**. Just ask around among your friends and colleagues what they know about the company. Your recruiter is a good resource, too.

Everything you find out from this process will help you be so much better in the phone interview. You'll be more comfortable, you'll be more confident, you'll answer all their questions better, and you'll make it much more likely to move forward to the face-to-face.

"The key to success is to focus our conscious minds on things we desire, not things we fear."
–Brian Tracy

Phone Interview Tips - #8

Research the Interviewer

Why research the interviewer before your phone interview? Because the job interview is a sales process in which you are both the product and the sales rep. One of the first rules of sales is "Know Your Customer." You will sell more effectively if you know a little something about the person buying the product.

What Should You Search For?

You need some basic background on this person, such as:

- Where are they from?
- How did they come up in the business?
- Is their background similar or different than yours?
- What companies have they worked for?
- What hobbies do they have?

Finding these answers will help you with two important things:

1) Establishing rapport

   Maybe you're from the same part of the country, or maybe you share a hobby. Or maybe you definitely don't—if you find out that your interviewer is a member of PETA, you won't want to talk about your love of hunting.

2) Tailoring your interview answers

   The interviewer's career background might provide some clues as to what he or she values. If you can talk about things in your own background you know they'll value, that will give you an advantage in the process.

Use LinkedIn to Research the Interviewer

LinkedIn profiles are invaluable sources of information.

- What jobs have they had?
- What groups are they in?
- What things to they talk about in their status updates?

All these things can give you important clues that will help you in your conversation.

Use Facebook to Research the Interviewer

Since Facebook is more of a social site than LinkedIn, you're going to be able to get another, more personal perspective on your interviewer:

- What do they post?
- What do they think is funny?
- Do they hold strong political views?

This research will make you feel more comfortable speaking with this person because you won't be going in cold. Being more comfortable means also being more confident.

Why Phone Interviews Are Like Coffee Dates

A phone interview is a little like setting up a date though an online dating service. You like the profile, but the safe thing to do is meet for coffee to see if your date is normal or bat-crap crazy. Dinner is too much of a commitment yet. Interviews follow the same logic. Phone interviews are the coffee date, face-to-face interviews are dinner.

Know What They'll See
When They Research You

Recruiters and hiring managers will look for you online as a part of their research into you as a candidate. They will make judgments on what they find and they may ask you about it in your phone interview. Will anything especially impressive (or questionable) show up about you? To know what they will see when they search your name, search your own name first.

Use Google, Yahoo, and Bing. Put quotes around it, like "John Smith" or "Jane Jones". Using the quotes means that your search results will be more focused and relevant for you.

Know what's there, and be prepared to discuss it.

Prepare Answers
to Common Phone Interview Questions

It's simple: The more prepared you are for your phone interview (or any interview), the better impression you'll make.

Have great answers ready for these common phone interview questions, and boost your chances of moving forward.

Tell me about yourself.

This question really means, "Tell me something that will matter to me as I consider you for this job." So, always focus on your key professional "selling points."

Briefly mention your degree or any relevant classes you've taken, and then go into your background: promotions, awards, or key accomplishments that matter to your future success at this job.

You can say something along the lines of, "I have a degree in X, and over the last couple of years I've added classes in Y to round out my knowledge base. I started out at ABC Corporation, and moved to the Acme Company, where I achieved XYZ, and was promoted 3 times and received an award for X." Or whatever you can say that sums up your education, background, and significant accomplishments.

You don't need to talk longer than a minute or so—just deliver a targeted message that says: "I am skilled, I have accomplished some great things, and I can bring that to work here for you."

Why are you interested in this job?

Your company research should help you answer this question. Tell them why your skills are a good fit, and then give about 3 reasons why you'd like working at this company. How will it benefit you personally and professionally?

Always keep this answer **positive**. Talk about how great this company is and what makes you enthusiastic about working there. Focus on why you're looking forward to this opportunity and using your skills in X, Y, and Z to succeed in this job.

Here's an example:

"Based on the research I've done, I was very impressed with your track record in X and your plans for Y. This company is a place where my background in ABC and my strengths in XYZ can be put to great use. I can make the kind of contributions you need to achieve the company's goals, and that's exciting for me."

See? You're not talking about how the company can help you develop or get further in your career. That's what **you're** going to get out of it, and they don't care. Tell them what **they're** going to get out of this deal—someone whose skills can help them reach **their** goals. Tell them the benefits of hiring you.

Why are you leaving your current job?

This can be a difficult question, because you never want to be negative in any job interview answer—however, most people don't leave a job that's a positive situation. Never, ever say anything like, "Because I can't stand it there anymore."

Try to answer this question by focusing on why *this* job appeals to you, rather than why your last one doesn't anymore. If you must give a reason, try to choose one that was a factor in your old job that won't be in this one (location, commute, or something else that's a "neutral" answer).

For instance, if this job requires no travel, say, "There's a lot of travel in the old job and I'm ready to be in my own bed more often."

Or if you're moving from a small company to a big one: "I've loved my time at XYZ company and learned many things, but there's just not as much room for growth as I'd like."

Be as brief as you can. Mostly what you want to do here is focus on how it's not that you're running **from** that job, it's that you're running **to** this job. This job is such a great fit, and offers so many things you're looking for, and so on...

"Believe in yourself! Have faith in your abilities! Without a humble but reasonable confidence in your own powers you cannot be successful or happy."
–Norman Vincent Peale

One Caution About Preparing Answers Ahead of Time...

Even though you have these great prepared answers, be careful not to just read them out loud. Some people cannot do this naturally and sound like they're reading something out loud, which is bad. Either practice ahead of time so you sound smooth and natural, or just jot down a few notes and phrases to incorporate into your on-the-spot answer.

Phone Interview Tips #11

Prepare Answers
to Tricky Phone Interview Questions

Here's a secret...every job interview answer can trip you up, but I often see candidates make mistakes with these:

What are your weaknesses?

As in all job interview answers, YOU have the power to mold and shape this answer into one that serves you best (while sticking to the truth, of course).

There are several approaches you can take, but this is the one I think will help you most:

Choose a real weakness that might cause you a problem in other areas of your life but actually helps you achieve in this job. (Just don't choose perfectionism, because it's too much of a cliché.)

For instance, I always used impatience as my weakness. No one can argue that impatience isn't a real weakness—it is, and it's caused me problems. Impatience is also something that's driven me to succeed faster than other people.

Someone else could answer that they get frustrated with people who don't work as quickly as they do—which says that you work fast and are dedicated.

Thinking about the greatest weakness question this way requires a little more creativity and thoughtfulness on your part, but the strategic advantages you'll gain from it in your interview will be worth it.

What are your strengths?

To answer this question, think about the things this hiring manager is looking for: skill sets, relationships, background, character traits...everything that is necessary to be successful in this role, and include these things (as they pertain to you) in your answer.

Maybe this job is going to be an incredible amount of work—so point out your work ethic. Maybe it's going to require tremendous communication skills—give an example of yours. Maybe it requires a quick learning curve—so say why you're going to be able to get up to speed quickly. Maybe it requires a particular background, and you have that.
Know how your skill set equals the skill set required for this position, and then deliver a concise but detailed statement that explains that. Show them that you fit. And provide a few examples of how you have done that in the past (which means that you can do it again for them). What have you achieved or accomplished that make you a great fit for

this role?

Always tie your answer to your fit for the job.

When could you start?

The best answer to this is "I can start right away" or "I have to give my current company two weeks' notice, so I could start as soon as two weeks after I accept a written offer."

If you don't answer this directly, you could look like you're not serious about this job, and get knocked out of the running for it.

Are you willing to relocate?

If your answer is "Yes," you have no issue. If you're not sure, the knee-jerk answer many people give ("I'd consider it for the right opportunity") is not your best answer because it puts your motivation for wanting the job more into the 'money' category rather than the 'fulfilling work / great fit' category. It's a subtle but important distinction that will take the shine off your candidacy if you say it. What can you say?

If you're a 'No'...

If your answer is unequivocally 'no', you have to say so. It's only going to cause you problems if they do end up offering you the job and you won't move. (Although, let me just say that life can turn on a dime. What looks like "never" right now might not look like that in a few months or a year.) If you really want this job, and you can't move immediately, say so. But consider saying something like, "I'd rather not move right now, but you never know what tomorrow will bring. And I'm very interested in this position and this company."

If you're a 'Maybe'...

You'd rather not commit to packing up your entire life just yet, but you don't want this job to slip away because of it. Try something like, "I'm interested in growing my career, and if relocating for the job is a necessary part of that, of course I'd consider it." That doesn't commit you to moving. It just confirms that your career (and this job) is important—and it's tactful.

These answers don't commit you to anything, but they do help you appear to be more sincere, flexible, tactful, and reasonable than "I'd consider it for the right opportunity." They keep the conversation going in a positive direction, which is a big plus for any job interview.

Where do you see yourself in 5 years?

In other words, are you going to bail on them in a few months for another job, or are you going to stick around and make their training and investment in you pay off? Is this a stepping stone on your career path, or is this a job to pay the bills until you can do what you really want to do?

Many, many people believe that the best answer is some version of: "I see myself in your job!" or, "I want to be in management" because they think it shows ambition. That is not always the best answer.

If you are interviewing with a very large company, it might be just fine to talk about your desire to be promoted and to grow within the company, because they have room for you to do that.

If you are interviewing with a small company, an answer like that might be considered a threat to this person's job. If they don't have anywhere to go, they're certainly not going to let you push them out.

A much better answer in both situations is to say something more along the lines of "I want to grow and develop my skills," or "I want to be all I can be." Talk about how you look forward to greater responsibility as you learn more about the company, and that you hope to be ready to do more things.

Then you can say, "if you are looking at me for a management position at that time, I would be interested in it, but that's not necessarily my end goal. What I really want out of this is to learn, to grow, and to contribute in a meaningful way."

There is no hiring manager who won't be impressed by a strategic job interview answer like that.

Advice for the Over 50 Candidate

If you're an "over 50" candidate, don't say that you'll be thinking about retirement. You want to give the impression that you are still looking forward to learning and growing and working, not looking forward to golf.

Phone Interview Tips #12

Have Stories Ready
for Behavioral Interview Questions

Hiring managers love behavioral interview questions, because they dig deeper into what kind of employee you really are. Answers to behavioral interview questions must be in the form of stories, or examples, from your career.

To answer behavioral interview questions well, come up with real life examples of how you have excelled in your work. Develop these stories for your behavioral interview.

A great way to organize your stories is with the STAR technique.

Begin with S, the "Situation", or T, "Task".

Give a little background into the problem you faced and set up the scenario. Provide some details about when and where it took place and some general context as to why it occurred. Explain what the situation required from you and what you did to resolve the issue.

Then comes A for "Action".

Tell what your options were and which one you chose, and explain to the interviewer what role you played in the outcome.

The last letter stands for "Results".

Emphasize the measurable results that wrapped up the situation in your favor. Be very specific about the results you personally achieved, what you learned and how your organization benefited from your part in the resolution.

With this structure, walk them through your thought process to show that you are strategic, thoughtful, knowledgeable, and can communicate well.

- How did you think about / approach that situation?

- Why did you choose that particular plan of action?

- How did you implement it?

- What happened?

- Did you have to adjust your approach?

- What did you learn from it?

- If you had to do it again, would you do it differently, and why?

Here are 3 examples for how to answer behavioral interview questions:

What do you consider to be your most significant accomplishment?

Don't just answer this by talking about the end result of your effort, as in "I ranked #1 among sales reps for 5 years in a row" or "I saved my company $5 million dollars last year." That's fantastic, but if you limit your answer like that, you're missing out on some prime selling time here.

Tell how you approached the problem or the goal and how you used the resources you had available. Talk about what obstacles you came up against and how you overcame them.

An Interviewer's Thoughts

Always focus your answer on work-related accomplishments.

I have interviewed too many well-meaning but clueless candidates who answered this question with, "My kids are my greatest accomplishment," or some other personal-life answer. That's a truly lovely sentiment, but it will not get you hired.

This answer should ALWAYS be a work-related accomplishment—especially, a work-related accomplishment that is relevant to the job you are currently applying for.

Have you ever had difficulty working with a supervisor or manager?

Be very careful when answering this question. Even if you had legitimate complaints about your old boss (and lots of bosses earn every one of those complaints), it's never a good idea to badmouth your former boss.

If possible, avoid it:

"I can't say that I've ever had trouble working with anyone. I appreciate the personality differences I've seen in my various supervisors and found that I learned something from working with each of those styles."

If you can't avoid it, tell the story along with your thought process. But keep in mind that any story you tell should be the Disney version—positive, with a happy ending.

For example, you could say something like:

"I did get off to a bad start with my manager in my very first job because we had different expectations and at the time, I didn't know enough to ask about those before I started work. But I got some very good advice to go talk with him about it, and we cleared the air. It turned out to be a great experience for me, and it was a good lesson to take forward in my career. Good communication is essential to a productive working relationship."

See? You haven't said anything negative about yourself or about your manager. It was the *situation* that was difficult. You took proactive steps to resolve it in a mature fashion, and the end result was a productive relationship.

How do you deal with stressful situations?

Every job has stress. Show that you can handle yours in a professional manner, possibly taking them through your thought process:

"If a situation seems overwhelming, I mentally break it up into smaller steps, or doable goals, and focus on reaching each one on the way to accomplishing the larger task. In fact, that's what I did with XYZ project. We had a major issue with X problem, but I broke it down into 'what needs to happen first,' and concentrated on one step at a time. I was able to see more solutions to the larger problem, and in fact, we got the entire project done in record time."

Or, *"I find it best do concentrate on remaining calm, maybe taking a few deep breaths. When I run into a customer who's upset, it helps them to calm down if I'm calm and we can work together to resolve the situation."*

Above all, choose an answer that shows that you can meet a stressful situation head-on in a productive, positive manner and let nothing stop you from accomplishing your goals.

Hint: *If you ever hear silence after you've finished an answer, or you get the feeling that you didn't quite hit the nail on the head, ask the interviewer: "Did that answer your question?" or "Was that what you were looking for?" or "Would you like more information?"*

How to Avoid the Salary Question

"What salary are you looking for?"

Some interviewers will ask you this. They are trying to find out if they can afford you (maybe because you're overqualified). Try to avoid answering. You never want to talk about money until they make you an offer. Depending on your personality and your individual situation, you've got a couple of good avoidance tactics:

1. **Be straightforward** and say, "I'm really interested in finding out more about the job and telling you more about me so that we can see if we're a good fit before we start talking about the money."

2. **Put them off.** Say, "I'm looking for a great opportunity, and I'm sure you'll offer a salary that's commensurate with the

responsibility of this job." This is a good, diplomatic answer.

If they push for a more specific answer, say something like,

"I'm sure that you're offering an appropriate range for this position, and it won't be a problem. What range have you budgeted for it?" (Turning the question back to them is one of my favorite tactics.)

Why is it so important to avoid answering this question?

Because you don't want to price yourself out of the job by naming something too high, and you don't want to shortchange yourself by naming something too low. Be sure to do salary research before your interview so you at least have a ballpark of what's appropriate for your experience level, in your area of the country.

Your ideal goal is to get them to want to hire you first—and *then* you talk about the money. If they don't want to hire you, the money doesn't matter anyway.

Be Positive!

When answering all job interview questions, keep your answers focused on the positive. Talk up your strengths as much as you can so that you sell yourself for the job.

Practice Your Phone Interview

How do athletes win championships? Practice.

How do you get better at interviews so you win the job ? Practice.

Interviewing well is not a talent—it is a **skill**. To get better at a skill, you have to practice.

Here's how to practice a phone interview:

Prepare answers for questions you'll probably be asked.

Several questions always get asked, like "Why are you interested in this job?" or "Tell me about yourself." They will want to talk about your basic skill sets, they'll want to go over your resume with you, and they want to know why they should be interested in talking more with you.

Having answers ready that you can deliver smoothly is very helpful.

But phone interviews are also where employers are looking for any knockout factors, or red flags. Anticipate questions about difficult situations in your past and come up with good answers to give. For instance:

If you've got an employment gap on your resume...

Put yourself in the shoes of this hiring manager. Think about what their greatest fears are with this—that you were fired for cause, or there's something wrong with you and that's why you haven't already been hired. Then think about what will make them feel better:

- If you were laid off, it will help a lot if you can tell them that you were part of a mass layoff, and that it wasn't just you—and that you've been taking your time to find the right job.

- If you can truthfully say that you took time off to deal with a family emergency, or to take care of your children, or to go back to school, all those things make sense, too.

- If you can provide strong references from people you have worked for, that is a big help. It reassures them that you were a good choice for someone else, and you will be for them, too.

Come up with an explanation that makes sense to them, and be confident when you explain it. Confidence covers a multitude of sins. If you're OK with it, it makes it easier for them to be OK with it. If you're nervous or apologetic, it makes them wonder what it is that you have to be guilty about. Be confident and make sure that your explanation addresses those fears of the hiring manager.

If you've been a job hopper....

Give a brief but reasonable explanation, and point out why this job would allow you to settle down for a while.

Rehearse your answers and explanations.

This is where the true practicing happens that will help you win the game. Rehearse your explanations and your answers either by recording yourself to see how you sound, or getting someone to role-play the interview with you and be your "interviewer." Through role-playing, you can get valuable feedback about not just the quality of your answers, but how you come across over the phone. Is your voice strong? Do you sound confident and enthusiastic? A friend can do this for you, or a career coach, or you can use Career Confidential's Job Interview Questions and Answers app.

It takes time to practice your answers, but the results will be worth it. You will be more confident in the phone interview, which will come across to the interviewer as competence, professionalism, and enthusiasm...all good things to help move you to the face-to-face.

"I'm a great believer in luck, and I find
the harder I work, the more I have of it."
–Thomas Jefferson

Build Your Confidence

The more confident you are, the more relaxed you'll be and the better interview you will have.

Use these **3 tips** to **build your confidence** so you can have a great phone interview:

1. Dress in a Killer Outfit

The clothes we put on have a major impact on how we behave. (I have a friend who's noticed that the days she wears her boots, she's got a little more strut in her step than if she's kicking around in her sneakers.) It is a proven fact that the clothes you wear affect your behavior.

Put on a suit that makes you feel not just professional, but fantastic. If you feel it, you will act it. It will come across even over the phone.

2. Be Prepared

Do all your pre-interview research, list out the questions you want to ask, and write down some key points you want to make. The more you do, the more prepared you will be and the more confident you will feel.

3. Be Organized.

Go old-school and lay out all your papers on your desk in front of you—your resume, your question list, your notes, everything. Don't just keep it on your computer screen so you have to click to find it—paper is the way to go. It's faster and more reliable. What if your computer freezes up? You can certainly have the company's website up, and maybe another site or two in other tabs, but for the most part, play it safe and keep your most important documents safely in front of you on your desk.

*"One important key to success is self-confidence.
An important key to self-confidence is preparation."
–Arthur Ashe*

Phone Interview Tips - #7

Get Your Cheat Sheets Ready

Cheat sheets are just what they sound like: notes that help you do better on the test, which in this case is the phone interview. Phone interviews don't have many advantages for you, but this is a big one. Make the most of it with these cheat sheet ideas:

Your Resume

Always have your resume in front of you. In a phone interview, they will ask you questions about your resume. Highlight a few especially relevant lines on your resume so you can find them faster.

The Job Description

Print out the job description to keep in front of you, with notes for yourself of examples/stories of when you have done the things in the description.

A List of Questions to Ask

Asking questions is a powerful interview strategy. You'd be surprised at how many candidates just answer questions and don't take the initiative to ask any—and they're hurting themselves. Asking questions shows enthusiasm and asking the right ones will give you a lot of helpful information you wouldn't otherwise get.

A few good questions to ask:

- Why is this job open?
- How long was the last person in this position?
- When do you expect to have someone hired?
- What are the biggest challenges of this position?
- How do you plan to deal with X? (X is whatever is appropriate for your field—do your research.)
- When can I expect to hear from you about next steps?

Key Points You Want To Make About Yourself

You should have a few key 'selling' points that make you a great fit for this job, and you need to make sure that you mention them. Write them down so you won't forget.

Also, write down the terms you want to use to describe yourself. If you have a certain phrase or wording that describes you in a powerful way, write it down so you will remember to say it that way.

Written-Out Answers To Interview Questions

You can always anticipate a few interview questions:

- Tell me about yourself.
- Why are you interested in this job?
- Why are you leaving your current job?

Jot down some good answers to these standard questions so you're ready. Just don't read it word for word. It should sound natural.

Keep A Pen And Paper So You Can Take Notes

Take notes throughout your conversation. It will help you write a more intelligent and customized thank you note, and it will help you better prepare for your face-to-face interview. And, if they ask you to write down a website or a phone number, you will be able to do that quickly.

"Opportunities don't often come along.
So, when they do, you have to grab them."
–Audrey Hepburn

Cheat Sheet Hint:

You want to print out hard copies of your cheat sheets
just in case your internet fails....plus, it's quieter to look at

papers (if you're not shuffling) than to type or click around finding things on your computer.

Prepare to Be 'Screened'
--But Not Screened Out

Phone interviews are really phone *screens*. They're screening candidates to narrow down the list of who to invite for a face-to-face interview. Your job is to keep them from eliminating you. How?

(1) Follow good phone interview practices:

- Make sure you've got a quiet room with no distractions.
- Research the company.
- Practice answering typical phone interview questions.
- Communicate enthusiasm.
- Be positive all the way through your conversation.

(2) Help them see that it would be feasible to hire you:

- Are you in the right **location**? If so, great. If not, mention any plans you might have for moving to that location. If you don't need relocation help, that can be a big plus.

- How fast will you be **available**? That's totally up to your own situation, but generally, sooner is better.

- Do you **understand the job**? Are you very clear on what the job will entail?

Third, be ready to talk about your resume:

- **Be prepared to give more detail** about your bullet points, and don't say anything that contradicts your resume.

- **Are there any worrisome parts of your resume?** Are you currently out of work? Do you have a big employment gap? Have you had too many jobs over the years? Be ready to explain all your jobs and transitions—and keep it positive. If something was a problem before (family issues, health problems, etc.), point out that it is resolved and you are ready to devote your time and effort to this job.

Throughout the call, they're going to be listening to what you say and how you say it, looking for a reason not to like you. Don't give them one. Be aware of any red flags of yours that might catch their attention, like less experience or employment gaps or job hopping, and come up with a positive answer before they ask you about it. Be upbeat, answer all their questions concisely but completely, show interest, ask questions, and be polite.

*"Whenever you are asked if you can do a job, tell 'em, 'Certainly I can!' Then get busy
and find out how to do it."*
–Theodore Roosevelt

Phone Interview Tips - #18

Biggest Phone Interview Mistakes

For such a short conversation, phone interviews are a surprisingly wide-open opportunity for screw-ups. Here are 9 ways to make a fatal phone interview mistake:

Failing to Prepare

If it isn't clear that you found out something about the company and the job before this call, they will assume that you are not very interested in it.

A Noisy Environment

This is an important meeting, and you should treat it as such. Be respectful of the interviewer and yourself by making the effort to set aside time and a quiet place for this call. Don't let any distractions keep you from being your best.

Talking on a Cell Phone with Poor Reception

If you can, always use a landline. If you must use a cell phone, be certain you have crystal-clear reception *before* your call—call a friend to make sure.

Drinking Water with Ice (Or Anything with Ice)

While it's good to have a glass of water nearby to keep your voice from getting scratchy, it's a bad idea to put ice in it. Over the phone, clinking ice is distracting and tends to make your listener think you're drinking alcohol. I don't know why, but that is the image that will show up in their mind's eye, and it will hurt you.

Keeping a Poker Face

If you don't smile when you speak during your conversation, it comes across to your interviewer as disinterest in the job, or even downright unfriendliness. Even if it's not a completely genuine emotion on your part, a smile will still communicate confidence, enthusiasm, and likeability.

Chewing Gum

Smacking in your interviewer's ear is a great way to get them to delete your name from the list. It's distracting, and it's rude. (Plus, what if you accidentally inhale it? That coughing fit won't really add to your professional image...) Spit out the gum.

Smoking

Listen to someone smoking a cigarette sometime....those long pauses with each drag, the hard exhales blowing out the smoke, the occasional coughs...and you'll understand why you don't want that in your conversation. For some interviewers, the fact that you smoke might be enough to knock you off the list—and you'll never know.

Driving

Never interview while driving. That tells them that you aren't taking this opportunity seriously enough to devote time to it, and you will be seriously distracted. Not only will you not have a good phone interview, you increase your chances of having an accident.

Using Your Speakerphone Function

Even if your intentions are good—like, you only want to put them on speakerphone so you can take notes—the result of putting them on speakerphone is bad. The sound quality of your call goes way, way down. They will hear any little background noise, and it will be distracting. When they realize you have them on speakerphone, their immediate reaction will be a negative one: "this person is not professional," "this person is not focusing their full attention on this call," "this person doesn't care about this job opportunity."

Bringing Up Any Concerns You Have About This Job

Even if you have valid concerns about commute time, health benefits, or the company itself, this is not the time to bring it up. Any negativity puts a damper on the whole conversation. Even if it turns out that there's no problem and it will be wonderful, they will feel differently about you if you bring up concerns this early in the process. Just wait.

Pay attention to the details in your phone interview. The smallest actions can make the biggest impact on your call. It all affects whether or not you get to the face-to-face interview.

"Fall seven times, stand up eight."
–Japanese proverb

Phone Interview Etiquette

In any job interview, it's important to use your best manners—and telephone interviews are no exception. Besides your resume, this is their first impression of you. Make it a great one by being super-polite and professional. Here's how:

Answer the Phone with Your Name

Don't just say "Hello." Say, "Hello, this is John Smith." Answering the phone with your name helps the interviewer feel immediately comfortable that they have the right person on the line.

Address the Interviewer by Name

Make sure you know the name of your interviewer before you speak to them, even if you have to call and find out from someone else. It's much nicer to be able to say, "Hi, Mr. Smith" if you can.

Address the Interviewer Formally

Always address the interviewer as "Mr." or "Ms." So-and-So until you are told otherwise. Until they specifically say, "Please call me John," you may not address them by their first name.

Don't Interrupt

No matter how excited you are about the job, it's rude to interrupt while they are speaking. Wait for them to finish their question.

Don't Put Them On Speakerphone

Speakerphones convey the impression that you have something more important you need to be doing right now, and you're going to do it while you talk.

Turn Off Phone Features That Might Interrupt You

Call waiting, or anything else that might beep, buzz, or cause a blip in the conversation should be disabled for this call.

Respect Their Time

An important way to show that you respect the time of the person you're speaking with is to be very prepared for this interview. Research the company. Have questions prepared to ask. Know how you're going to answer at least the most typical interview questions so you can answer them fairly quickly. (Taking a few seconds to think about your answer is fine on some questions, but not all.) Have your resume, as well as all your notes, right in front of you so you can see them easily. You don't want to shuffle papers, looking for something while you're on the call. While you're at it, make sure you have a pen and paper to take notes on during the call. You will need the notes for later, and you'll be ready just in case they want you to write something down.

Ask About the Next Step

Express your interest in the job by asking about what the next step will be. When will you speak in person about this opportunity? Don't wait for them to bring it up. They might not...maybe they're waiting for you to do it to see if you want it, or maybe they have a few doubts about you that you need to clear up. **Do not end the call without knowing what happens next.**

Send a Thank You Note

Follow up after your phone interview by emailing a thank you note to the person you spoke to. Thank you notes are always the polite thing to do, and they make you stand out from the other candidates. Why email? Because it's faster. A fast response time is a positive thing.

"Manners are a sensitive awareness of the feelings of others. If you have that awareness, you have good manners, no matter what fork you use."
- Emily Post

Phone Interview Tips - #20

Tips to Help You Relax

One of the easiest ways to make a good impression in your phone interview is to be calm, cool, and collected all the way through. Here are 4 tips that will help you relax and have a great phone interview.

Be Over-Prepared

Nothing calms nerves like being ready for anything. That means, don't just go to the company's website...read it carefully. Go to the company's LinkedIn page and Facebook page, if they have it. Google them for the latest news. Look at their competitors. The more you can learn ahead of time, the better off you'll be. Knowledge is power.

Arrive Early

Be ready to start your call at least 5 minutes before it's supposed to start. Be sitting in your quiet room with the door closed, your glass of water on the desk, all your cheat sheets spread out, doing some deep, relaxing breathing. When it's time for the interview, you will sound calm, cool, and collected. And if they try the tactic that some interviewers do of calling early to catch you off guard, you'll be ready for them. It will impress them.

Keep Your Cheat Sheets Handy

Cheat sheets are anything that will help you do better in the interview— your resume, your list of questions to ask, references, key points to make, and a few phrases you want to use to describe yourself. Spread them out in front of you so they are easy to find. You will feel comfortable knowing if you forget anything, it's right there for you.

Practice Relaxation Breathing

Take a deep breath, hold it for a few seconds, and let it out slowly. Do this a few times before your call. Relaxation techniques like this do wonders for slowing down your heart rate and giving you a feeling of calm and control. If you need to do it during the call, go ahead—but don't breathe hard into the phone. That could sound a little awkward!

"The future belongs to those who believe
in the beauty of their dreams."
–Eleanor Roosevelt

Tips to Help You Focus

To be successful in your phone interview, you need to be on your toes and focused on the call. It's easy to get distracted when you don't have eye contact with the person you're speaking with. They can tell if your attention is wandering (which is bad), and you can easily miss a word in a question and answer it wrong.

Here are tips to help you focus:

* Set up in a **quiet room with no distractions—no TV, music, or other people.**

- **Eat before your interview.** Food is fuel, and hunger pangs or blood sugar dips are a distraction.

- **Go to the bathroom.** You can't do your best thinking when all you can concentrate on is how bad you've 'gotta go'.

- **Wear comfortable clothing.** Dress professionally to put yourself in the right frame of mind, but be comfortable so you're not fidgeting with scratchy or too-tight clothing.

- **Keep your notes in front of you.** Keep your resume, your list of questions to ask, your notes on the company, and the important points you want to make about yourself laid out right in front of you. You don't want to be shuffling papers, trying desperately to find something in the middle of your call.

- **Breathe.** Just before your call, take a few minutes to do a few deep, relaxing breaths. You want to calm your nerves so you don't sound jumpy or jittery. Relax and you'll be able to focus.

"The key to success is to focus our conscious mind on things we desire, not things we fear."
–Brian Tracy

Expect a Positive Outcome

Expect your phone interview to go well. Visualize having a great conversation and getting invited for the face-to-face. Feel the happiness and enthusiasm you'll get from this success.

Visualization is a great tool. It can be extremely helpful in calming your nerves and putting to rest any self-doubt before the interview. If you expect a positive outcome, you will behave differently than if you don't. Your breathing will relax, your words will change, you'll project energy, your voice will sound more upbeat, you will project confidence, and so then your actual outcome will change.

"A positive attitude causes a chain reaction of positive thoughts, events and outcomes. It is a catalyst and it sparks extraordinary results."
—Wade Boggs

Phone Interview Tips - #23

Make Your Voice Phone Interview-Ready

Interviewers concentrate very hard on your voice in a phone interview: Do you sound alert? Confident? Enthusiastic? Are there any red flags they need to worry about?

They don't have much to judge you on when you're on the phone, so they focus on what they can—the words you say, how you say them, and the sound of your voice.

Warm Up Your Voice Before the Interview

An hour or so before your interview, talk to someone else to warm up your voice. It's sort of like warming up before you work out. You want to

---

hit your speaking stride for that conversation, not sound scratchy or worse—sleepy—when you talk. If necessary, drink some hot tea with honey to smooth out your voice before the call.

A Fun Voice Warm-Up Tip

*If you like to sing, warm up your voice with a song.
Choose one that pumps you up and makes you feel fantastic
so it not only warms up your voice, but ramps up your
energy level before the call.*

Get a Glass of Water

Set a glass of water close by during your interview. Every so often, take a quick drink to keep your voice smooth. (But remember—no ice.)

Convey Enthusiasm with Your Tone

Aim for **positive, upbeat, energetic, and enthusiastic.** You don't have to be Perky Pamela if that's not your natural personality, but remember that this interview could be the beginning of a beautiful new job. That's a good thing, and you should act like it.

Speak Smoothly

Don't get flustered and tongue-tied. Practice your answers before the interview so that you are comfortable delivering them, and if necessary, slow down your speech so you don't trip yourself up.

The Deadliest Phone Interview Speech Sin

Please make sure you don't use irritating speech fillers like "um" and "uh." Taking a second or two to pause before your answer is much better than filling it with those.

"Big jobs usually go to the men who prove their ability to outgrow small ones."
–Ralph Waldo Emerson

Establish Rapport

People hire people they like, and that they connect with. For hiring managers to feel as though they like you and connect with you (and hire you), you need to establish rapport. How?

Greet them by name

People like to hear the sound of their own names. When you answer the phone (with, "Hello, this is Jane Smith"), and they say, "This is Susan Jones of Acme Company," you say, with warmth in your voice: "Hi Ms. Jones! I'm so glad to speak with you today!" or something similar that includes their name and expresses your enthusiasm.

Match the interviewer's energy and style of conversation

As the interviewer begins speaking, listen to how they sound: Are they warm and friendly? Matter of fact? Calm and low-key? Whatever it is, try to match it in your own voice. Don't mimic them and don't put on a 'fake' personality; just coordinate with them.

If you don't, you'll sound "off." If the interviewer is cheerleader bouncy, and you're matter of fact, you'll seem to that person as if you are uninterested in the job. Project some enthusiasm. If the interviewer is snappy and to-the-point, and you're so warm and friendly that you elaborate too long on your answers, the interviewer won't take you seriously for the job. Find out what 'page' they're on, and get on it with them.

Mention things you have in common

If you and the interviewer graduated from the same school, know the same people, or have read the same book lately (all of which you should know from researching the interviewer), mention it.

Deliver a sincere compliment

It's human nature to be attracted to people who compliment you, but an obviously fake, 'suck up' kind of compliment is worse than no compliment at all. If you find something in your research about this person or the company that truly impresses you, mention it.

Participate in the conversation

Do more than just answer the questions you're asked. Listen to what they're saying so you can ask intelligent, insightful follow up questions. Ask questions about the job, the company, and how they see your role or primary tasks.

Look at a photo of your interviewer (maybe)

It might help you to look at the smiling face of your interviewer that you find on their LinkedIn profile or company website so that you feel more connected and comfortable.

Phone Interview Tips - #25

Speak Positive Body Language (Yes, Even On the Phone)

Even though your interviewer can't see you, using the right body language in your phone interview will give you a better outcome.

Smile

It's amazing what smiling does to the sound of your voice. You sound friendlier and more confident.

Stand Up

You will project more energy if you stand up while you talk than if you sit, and you will actually feel more powerful and confident.

Walk Around (Maybe)

If you have a headset, walking around while you talk is a great way to make yourself more comfortable in a phone interview. Your feet spend some of the nervous energy that might come out through your voice—but don't walk around so much that you end up out of breath. That won't sound good on the other end of the line at all.

Follow Your Mother's Advice and Sit Up Straight

If you are more comfortable sitting for your interview, make sure you sit up straight with good posture and don't slump in your seat. Slumping will make you sound tired and uninterested in the job. Sitting up straight ensures that you sound attentive and interested. You'll breathe better, which will make you sound better.

Practice Relaxed Body Language

What you do physically while you're on the phone will show up in your voice. If you're sitting there all tensed up, you'll sound tense. If your arms are crossed, you'll sound just a little less friendly. Sit (or stand) with a relaxed, comfortable posture and it will help you sound like you are relaxed and comfortable with the interviewer.

Don't Fidget

Movement is good; fidgeting is not. Nervous habits will not help you feel more relaxed in the interview, and may even be distracting to the interviewer. Tapping your pen on the desk, tapping your foot, drumming your nails on the table...these are all attention-diverters. They will give away your nervousness and make the interviewer think you're not confident in your ability to do the job.

Make Them Like You—
Project Interest in and Enthusiasm for the Job

What hiring manager doesn't want to choose someone who is sincerely enthusiastic and excited about the job? They all do. If you're excited about the job, you'll try harder and do better than someone who isn't. Plus, your genuine enthusiasm will make them like you more. If they like you, they'll be more likely to hire you.

Here are **6 tips for projecting enthusiasm** in phone interviews:

Smile

Always smile while talking. Even though they can't see your smile, it will show up in your voice. You will sound warmer, friendlier, and more enthusiastic.

If you need reminders, sometimes it helps to keep a **mirror in front of you to remind yourself to smile. If that's what it takes, do it.

Be Animated

If you talk with your hands normally, then talk with your hands (even though they can't see you). If you want to walk around while you talk, do it. In fact, standing while you talk can lend you power and confidence.

Ask Questions

Ask about the process, the job, and the company. All your questions should be based on your research—not questions that could be answered in the job description or by Google.

Thank the Interviewer for Speaking With You

Always thank the person for taking the time to speak with you while you're on the call. After the call, send your thank you note.

Tell Them You're Interested

Don't assume the hiring manager knows you're interested in the job. It should be obvious (because why else would you be bothering with this interview?), but it really isn't. They might think you're on the fence about it...so going forward with you might be a waste of time. So tell them how much you're interested in the job.

Don't Talk Too Much

What happens if you talk too much or reveal too much information? Both show poor communication skills that could keep you from getting invited to the face-to-face.

Knowing how much to talk really depends on your interviewer. If they're talking a lot, it's OK to listen and see what you can learn. If they ask a lot of questions, you talk. As long as it feels like a back-and-forth conversation and not a monologue, you're probably good.

Don't spend too much time on an answer. A minute or two should be plenty. Practice your answers ahead of time to make sure they are succinct and focused.

While you're watching how much you talk, also watch what you say. Here are a few ways to avoid offering Too Much Information:

Keep your answers job-focused.

Many job seekers offer up personal information out of nervousness, an attempt to bond with the interviewer, or because they don't understand how to answer interview questions. For instance, when they hear "Tell me a little about yourself," they say things like, "I have two kids," or "I'm a Facebook junkie." Don't say those things. Your answer should always be, "I have a degree in X," "I have experience in Y," or something that relates to the job.

Don't be negative.

Negativity of all kinds is "too much information." Don't talk trash about your last job or boss. Don't talk about any personal problems (that's a double-whammy....personal AND negative). Don't even talk about things you don't like. Keep it positive.

Don't reveal your concerns about this job.

If you are worried about the salary or the hours or the travel requirements, DO NOT bring it up at this point. Even if there's no problem, expressing your concern will make you seem like a negative person, and it will be a mark against you.

"Be interesting, be enthusiastic
...and don't talk too much."
-Norman Vincent Peale

Listen Well

The art of conversation requires that you not only express yourself well, but also that you listen well. Good listeners are valued. Being a good listener means that you're going to have a more productive, higher-quality conversation than you would otherwise.

How can you be a good listener in a phone interview?

- **Create a quiet space for your interview.** You can't listen well if you can't hear what they are saying to you. This conversation is a priority, so treat it like one.

- **Pay attention.** Don't let yourself get distracted by ANYTHING.

Don't try to conduct it in a restaurant, while driving, or anywhere near a child or a pet. And try not to be thinking about what you're going to say while they are talking. You could easily miss something important.

- **Don't interrupt.** Assertiveness is fine in an interview; rudeness is not. Don't interrupt your interviewer, ever. If they mention something that confuses you or raises a question for you, write it down to ask when it's your turn.

- **Take notes.** As your interviewer talks, take notes on what he or she is saying. This will help you when you're asking questions, it will help you write a better thank you note, and it will help you prepare for the face-to-face interview. They might even ask you to write down a phone number or website. If you've been taking notes, you can do it without missing a beat.

- **Ask follow up questions.** Asking relevant follow up questions is a powerful way to show that you are listening and you are interested.

- **Clarify for understanding.** If the interviewer asks you a question and you're not sure what they want to know, ask. Blindly launching into an answer that turns out to be wrong is much worse than saying, "Do you mean X, or Y?"

Watch Your Language

Pop quiz: When you answer questions in a phone interview, which answer would hurt you the most?

(A) "Um...I'm not sure..."
(B) "I hated to leave that job. My boss was my BFF."
(C) "That customer was a pain in the @$$, but I won him over."
(D) All of the above.

The correct answer is (D).

In job interviews, the language you use can make or break your chances—and that's even more true in a telephone interview, where your voice is all they have to focus on. Your conversation must be professional. That means:

- **No using "um", "uh," or other speech fillers.** If you need to stop and think before you answer, then stop and think. A pause is fine. Nervously filling that pause with "umm...." Is not. It's distracting and chips away the professional image you're trying to project. Most people use speech fillers like "um," "uh," "you know" and "like" more than they realize—especially in high-pressure situations like interviews. Record yourself answering interview questions so you can determine if you need to work on eliminating those very annoying speech fillers.

- **No weak language.** Weak words and phrases will kill your offer because they cast doubt on your ability to do the job. I coach candidates all the time to avoid saying things like, "I think," "I hope," "with luck," or "if it goes well." Some people qualify their statements with phrases like these because they don't want to seem cocky. But what they're really doing is making themselves seem weak and not up to the job. Practice saying, "I can," "I will," and "I do." That shows confidence. Confidence is appealing.

- **No slang.** Avoid using slang words or expressions. It doesn't make you look young or hip; it just makes you look unprofessional. You should be putting your best foot forward in the interview, and that includes your language.

- **No questionable language.** Never, ever use swear words in an interview, even mild ones. I once had a candidate (because she was nervous) say "crap" 3 times in her interview—and she lost the job. Use your best manners.

- **No sarcasm.** Avoid sarcasm and jokes in phone interviews. Even if you feel you must break the ice, don't do it with a joke. They can't see your facial expression or body language, so you can't be sure that what you mean is what they hear. Play it safe.

It can be more difficult than you think to watch your language in an interview. A lot of these things just roll right off our tongues without us even thinking about it. And when we're in a high-pressure situation like an interview, it happens even more.

Your best bet to avoid these issues is to practice answering interview questions, or role-play your interview with a friend or an interview coach. The practice will help you be more aware of what you do so you can fix it, and it will help you be more comfortable so you don't slip up.

*"Never say anything about yourself
you do not want to come true."*
–Brian Tracy

Watch Your Tone

To speak confidently in any business situation, but especially on the phone, pay attention to the tone you use.

One of the worst tone offenders is the person who always ends a statement on a higher note, so that it sounds like a question. This is a sure-fire way to undermine your own authority and credibility. End your sentences on a lower note. You will sound more confident, so then you can inspire their confidence in you.

Overall, strive for polite, warm, and friendly—try to imagine that you're speaking with someone you already know and like.

Take Advantage of the Fact That They Can't See You

Even though phone interviews present challenges, they also present a few advantages that you can work with to make the most of it. Besides keeping all your notes (cheat sheets) out in front of you, here are **4 secret tricks** you can use to take advantage of your phone interview situation and overcome some common obstacles:

1. Look at a picture of your interviewer during the call.

Establishing rapport can be difficult because you can't see the interviewer's face. So, you might try setting up a photo of the interviewer to look at while you talk to feel more at ease. You can probably find their photo on their LinkedIn profile.

2. Look in the mirror —or not.

I've seen two competing schools of thought on the mirror issue:

One says, "Keep a mirror in front of you so you remember to smile while you talk"—and it is important to smile and stay relaxed, because that comes through in your voice. A mirror is a visual reminder, so you can easily see if you start to frown or tense up.

The other says, "Never look in a mirror while you talk because it will make you self-conscious and you'll sound stiff."

I think you should try it both ways in practice conversations and see which one works for you.

3. Stand up.

In a regular interview, you're sitting across from the interviewer. In a phone interview, you obviously have the choice about whether to stand or sit. In my opinion, you should stand. People tend to sound more energetic when they stand up, and their voices are stronger because they aren't slumped over in a chair. So, show your energy and enthusiasm by standing up!

4. Have the internet open and ready to use.

Just in case, keep the company's website open on your computer, and set another window open to Google (or the search engine you use). If you run across something you need to know right now, you can find it— but never, ever let them hear you typing.

In a phone interview, you actually have a lot of leeway to do what is going to make you feel more comfortable and confident. Use every advantage you can think of to do well in the phone interview and get to the face-to-face.

Questions You Should Ask

In every interview (phone or face-to-face), it is critically important to ask questions. Why?

(1) It makes you seem **engaged and interested** in the job.

(2) It makes you seem more **intelligent**—IF you ask good questions. (Don't ask questions you could easily find the answers to on Google.)

(3) It gives you a **strategic advantage**—ask good questions, and you find out what the interviewer really cares about.

What questions should you ask?

- *Why is this position open?*

This answer can give you all kinds of information you can't get anywhere else. Maybe the last employer was a poor performer. Why? Maybe they were promoted. Is that a typical career path in this company?

- **How long was the last person in this position?**

Their answer to this tells you about the turnover rate for the job. If they name a very short term, your follow-up question should be, "Why? Is that typical?" You want to know if there was a performance issue, a fit issue, or some other issue that might rear up to bite you when you're on the job.

- **What are the biggest challenges of this position?**

If you know their biggest problems, you can talk about how you can solve them.

- **How would you describe a typical day on the job?**

First, their answer will give you tremendous insight into whether or not you want to work there. Second, what they say will give you big clues to what they see as the most important tasks for that job, and what they're looking for you to do. These clues will help you tailor the rest of what you say to most effectively sell yourself for that job.

These questions uncover information, show your professionalism and interest in the job, and move you forward another step in the process. Ask these kinds of questions and you'll have a great phone interview.

Phone Interview Tips - #33

Questions You Should NEVER, EVER Ask

It's important to ask questions in your phone interview—but here are 9 questions you should never, ever ask.

1. "What does your company do?"

The only time this might ever be acceptable is if you are surprised by a telephone interview sneak attack—in other words, they call you up out of the blue and want to conduct your interview right there, right then. Otherwise, you've got time to prepare. Use it to research the company and find out what they do. Then you can focus your conversation on how you would be a great addition to their organization.

2. "Can you hang on while I take this call?"

This phone call is THE most important conversation you could possibly be having right now. Never allow other callers to interrupt. In fact, turn off call waiting, text alerts, or anything else that might beep and distract you during this call.

3. "I'm worried about...."

Even if you're very concerned about some factor in this new job (the commute, the transition, the hours, whatever), never, ever bring it up in the phone interview. It's just too soon. Bringing up something negative too early just makes *you* look negative. I've seen firsthand how fast job seekers get knocked out of consideration by bringing up problems before they should.

4. "What's the salary range for this position?"

Never, ever bring up money at any point in the interview process—not until you have an offer in your hand.

5. "How much vacation time would I get?"

Nothing more clearly says, "What's in it for me?" than asking about benefits and perks. That's always a bad move. The job interview is a sales process—you are the product and the sales rep. That interviewer is your customer—which means your focus must be on what's in it for *them*. Once you've convinced them that you are the right person to hire, then you can talk about what you're getting out of it—and you can decide if you're interested or not at that point.

6. "How much overtime is required?"

You don't even have the job yet, and you're complaining about the hours? No one wants to be chained to their job, but asking about hours this soon makes it seem like you'll work as little as you can get away with.

7. "Do I have to pass a drug test or background check?"

Nothing says "I do illegal drugs" like "Do I have to take a drug test?" Ditto for the background check—they will suspect you have something to hide.

8. "What kind of health insurance do you offer?"

Not that this isn't an important question, but there's a time and a place, and this isn't it. This question plants the seed that you have some medical issues (chronic illness, pregnancy plans) that will cause you to miss work.

9. "Will I be able to work from home?"

When they hear this question, they won't picture you actually working from home....they'll picture you *saying* you're working while you're at the racetrack, getting your nails done, watching TV, whatever...a nightmare waiting to happen.

The One Question You Absolutely Must Ask, No Matter What

One question will improve your interview performance more than any other. What's the question? It's:

What does your ideal candidate look like?

What's on their ultimate wish list of skills and qualifications of someone in this role? If a person with those qualities walked through the door, they'd hire them on the spot.

You might say, "Why should I ask about their perfect candidate? I'm not perfect. Won't it make me look bad?" No, it won't. In fac,t it will help you.

Odds are very good that their ideal candidate is not going to show up— because it's an ideal. So what's the point of asking about it?

Their answer tells you what they really care about. It's like asking (without saying directly), *"What would you really like to hear from me in this interview? What can I say to you that will get me this job?"* That is POWERFUL information. With this knowledge, every interview answer you give for the rest of the interview can be geared to what will appeal to them most.

When should you ask this question? Ask it fairly early in the interview, before you start to get too deep in talking about yourself.

Does it have to be those exact words? No. Use whatever words are comfortable for you:

- *Tell me about your ideal candidate.*
- *If you had a checklist for a perfect candidate, what would be on it?*
- *What are the qualities of someone who would be perfect in this role?*

It should feel like a natural part of your conversation, so ask it however it works for you.

Do you really have to ask this? Yes.

Can't you just go by what the job description says? No. It's possible that someone besides the person interviewing you wrote the description—so maybe it's not completely accurate. It's too much of a gamble for this important conversation.

What do you do with this information? You use it to help tailor your answers to their interview questions.

If they ask about your proudest accomplishment, choose one that speaks to their wish list. You don't want to talk about something that they won't care about hearing.

If they ask why you think you'd be a good fit, then you can talk about the skills that match up with what they told you.

Every time they ask you a question, say something that answers that wish list as much as you can.

Delivering these types of super-targeted answers help you CRUSH the interview. It's being strategic and smart in how you approach the entire process. It will help push you along to getting the face-to-face interview.

"Do one thing every day that scares you."

—Eleanor Roosevelt

Before You End the Call...
Make Sure You've Hit Your Target Goal

The entire goal of your phone interview is to get to the face-to-face. The best way to get to that next step is to ask for it. So before you end this call, ask for a time to meet face-to-face to discuss this opportunity in more detail.

You could be direct and say,

"I am very excited about this opportunity. When can we get together to talk about this in greater detail?"

Or, "I'd really like to visit with you in person to show you what I can do for you. When can you meet with me?"

Or, "Based on what we've talked about, this sounds like a great fit for me and I am very interested in meeting with you to discuss it further. When can we schedule it?"

Or, "Thank you so much for speaking with me today. I am excited about this opportunity and think I would be a great fit. My skills in A, B, and C line up with what you said you were looking for. I would love to come in and talk with you in person about it. When can we schedule that?"

This is where the rubber meets the road. Many candidates will wait and hope to be invited because they don't want to seem too bold or desperate. That's a weak position to be in and won't help you. A few braver candidates will say, "When do you expect to make a decision?" That's a lot better, but not the best. **The bravest candidates who see the most success at getting to the next step** say something like, "I am really interested in this position. It sounds like a great fit. When can we meet to discuss this further?"

Asking "When can we meet?" is a great move because it either secures your interview, or it forces them to tell you they're not planning to bring you in. If that's the case, you can probably find out why they have doubts. Sometimes it's a real issue that you can't say anything to fix— but sometimes, it's a simple miscommunication that you can clear up right then. Once you clear it up, they feel comfortable with asking you to come in and interview. This simple question can be what gets you to the face-to-face interview.

If that's too much for you, at least ask about next steps, or the timeline:

"I am very interested in this job, and I would love to move forward. What are the next steps?" The best answer would be, "I want to set you up to come in." If they say, "I have more people to interview," ask

"What is your timeline for beginning face-to-face interviews?" At least this way you'll know when you can to expect to hear something, and you won't have to worry about it.

You need to know, before you hang up, what their expectations are for the next steps, what their timeline is, and what their process for getting all this done will be. They expect you to ask, and you deserve to know so you don't have to sit and wonder (and worry).

Also before you hang up, make sure you have the interviewer's contact information so you can send a thank you note. Aim for at least getting his or her email address.

If they invite you for the face-to-face interview during this call, thank them for the opportunity, and get all the details:

When and where is the interview?
Who will you interview with—what is their contact information?
When do they expect to have a final decision made?

Bottom line:

Before you end this call, know what is happening next.

"It is never too late to be what you might have been."
—George Eliot

Clarify, Clarify, Clarify

Job interviews are all about communication. You will only get the job if you can successfully communicate that you *understand* the job, that you *can* do the job, that you *will* do the job, and that you *pose no risk* to this person's continued employment. (That's why 30-60-90-day plans are such great job interview tools.) This requires good, clear communication.

The phone interview is the first step in this communication process— but there's a problem. Phone interviews mean that you can't see the person you're talking to. When you can't see them, your communication suffers. You have no handy facial expressions or gestures to read, so that cuts a big source of information. They can't see you, so your charming personality and winning smile is muffled. You can't show them your 30-60-90-day plan or your brag book. You only have your words and your voice.

This is why it is so important to clarify for understanding all the way through the interview:

Before the interview

Set yourself up for clear communications by controlling the time, place, and quality of your call.

Find out everything you can know before you start the interview.

During the interview

If you don't understand the question, don't answer it. Ask what they mean. You can put your foot in your mouth really quickly by plowing ahead and answering something you don't understand because you think they have to. If there's any doubt at all, ask. Say something like, "Do you mean X?" or "Are you referring to Y?" or "Are you asking about ABC?" You can't communicate well if you're not answering the question they asked.

Ending the interview

Do not hang up from this call without being clear about what happens next.

- Say, "I've really enjoyed talking to you. From what we've discussed so far, it sounds like a good fit to me. Do you agree?"

- Say, "Have I given you enough information so that you feel comfortable moving me forward in this process?"

You can say any number of things that make it clear that you want to move forward and ask if they agree with you.

If they're thinking of crossing you off the list, you need to find out

BEFORE they hang up. *That's* your chance to change their mind. Sometimes, it's a misunderstanding, an assumption they've made, or even just because you forgot to tell them something. If you can correct whatever it is, you've just saved your face-to-face interview.

Most job seekers would never dream of asking for this next step. Instead, they keep answering questions until the interviewer says something like: "Well, it was great talking to you. We've got a few more people to talk to. I'll be in touch." Know what that tells you? Nothing. You hang up not knowing if they liked you, if they're calling you back, if you're moving forward, nothing. Then you're stuck waiting, and waiting, and waiting. If the call doesn't come, that's when you find out they've screened you out. By then, it's too late to do anything about it. The time to act is during the interview.

Clarify, clarify, clarify. You deserve to know.

"Success doesn't come to you, you go to it."

–Marva Collins

Write a Thank You Note

How do you follow up after a phone interview? You follow up the exact same way you would after a face-to-face interview: send a well-thought-out, comprehensive, and timely thank you note.

Your thank you note should actually be a **thank you email.** Why an email? Because it's faster.

It's in your best interests to get your thank you note in their hands **within 24 hours** of your interview. Why? Because they will make decisions quickly about who to ask in for a face-to-face interview.

A good thank you note can easily tip the scales in your favor, and get you that invitation.

A good thank you note is a substantial one. Say much more than, "Thanks for interviewing me. I hope we can talk again."

Say (for example, depending on your conversation):

"Thank you for speaking with me today. I am very excited about this job and think I'd be a great fit. I really see how my skills and experience in X, Y, and Z can help you meet your ABC goals. My skills in D, E, and F would be an additional advantage. I am looking forward to meeting with you to talk more about it. I will call you on Wednesday to set it up. Sincerely..."

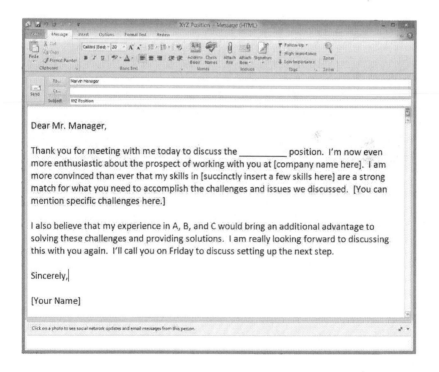

That kind of note does a lot of things for you. It shows your good manners, because you've thanked them for taking the time to talk to you. It shows your professionalism, because you're talking about how you can help them reach their goals. It reinforces the idea of you being a good fit by highlighting your skills. And it shows that you want the job because you're going to call to make sure you get a chance to discuss it. All good things.

Who should you send your email to? **Everyone you speak with deserves a thank you email.** If a recruiter set this up for you, send the recruiter a note, too. If the hiring manager arranged for you to speak with someone else, send that person a note AND send the hiring manager a note saying, "I spoke with so-and-so and it went well."

Even if your interview didn't go well, you should send an email. It's a chance for you to do some damage control. Address whatever you think the problem was and try to rectify it. Mention things you forgot to say that would be helpful to your cause. Correct any misconceptions. It might not work, but it could work and you should try.

"None of us got to where we are alone.
Whether the assistance we received was obvious or subtle,
acknowledging someone's help is a big part of understand-
ing the importance of saying thank you."
- Harvey Mackay

Send a thank you note even if you know you
are not moving forward.

Why? It lays the foundation for a potential positive outcome
to be determined in the future. Maybe they'll have another
position that's a better fit later on, maybe they'll recommend
you to someone else....you never know.

BONUS

Phone Interview Checklist

Want to be organized for your phone interview? Leave nothing to chance? Give yourself the best possible outcome? Then create a phone interview checklist like this one so you won't forget any vital detail.

o **Pick a good time and place** – The first thing you have to do when setting up a phone interview is to choose a good time for you, when you will be at your best (most alert), and then choose where to have this very important conversation. It must be somewhere quiet, where you will not be distracted. No pets, kids, or chatty people at the next table. Quiet.

o **Research the company** – Phone interviews aren't 'get-to-know-you' sessions—they're the first step toward getting an offer. Get to know them before your interview in your pre-interview research. Learning what you can about the company ahead of time signals that you are a professional, and that you are taking this opportunity seriously. It also allows you to come up with better interview answers as well as higher-quality questions of your own.

o **Research the interviewer** – What does the person who's interviewing you do at this company? Is it going to be your potential boss? Is it someone in HR? What is their background? What do they care about? Remember that the job interview is a sales process. This person is the customer, or the buyer. This is the one who's going to say 'yes' or 'no' to moving you to the next step. Find out what you can about your customer before you get there.

o **Prepare answers to common interview questions (and practice saying them)** – It's always a good idea to practice answering interview questions before any interview. Interviews are stressful. Take away some of the stress by knowing you have fantastic answers to "Tell me about yourself," "Why do you want to work here?" and other common questions.

o **Create a list of questions to ask** – Candidates are often asked, "Do you have any questions for me?" toward the end of the interview. It's a bad idea to say, "No." Come up with some intelligent, thoughtful questions to ask then and during the course of your conversation.

o **Get your 'cheat sheets' ready** – The best thing about phone interviews is that you can cheat. By 'cheat,' I mean that since they can't see you, you are free to keep all your notes in front of you. Keep a copy of your resume, your list of questions to ask, some key points you want to make about why they should hire you, your list of references, and anything else that will ensure you have a great telephone interview.

○ **Find a landline to use** – If you have access to a landline, use it rather than your cell phone. With a cell phone, there's always a chance (even a small one) of bad reception, dropped calls, and "Hello? Can you hear me?" kinds of issues. Make sure you have a smooth, worry-free experience with a very stable landline.

○ **Think about your voice** – The person on the other end of the line only has your voice to judge you on. Do you sound friendly? Professional? Competent? Confident? Think about projecting those qualities with your voice.

○ **Watch what you say** – You don't want to be giving only 'yes' or 'no' answers, but you also don't want to be delivering a speech with every answer. Keep your answers under a minute or two, and limit yourself to answering the question—don't joke, don't ramble, and don't give them too much information. (And don't ask about salary, vacation, or benefits.)

○ **Smile** – Remember to smile when you speak. All by itself, smiling helps you sound friendlier, more enthusiastic, and more confident. If you have to keep a mirror up in front of you to remember to smile, do it.

○ **Ask for the next step** – Don't get off the phone without asking when you can meet in person to discuss this opportunity in greater detail. They might not even realize how much you want this job unless you express your enthusiasm and ask for it.

"Nothing in the world can take the place of persistence. Talent will not; nothing is more common than unsuccessful men with talent. Genius will not; unrewarded genius is almost a proverb. Education will not; the world is full of educated derelicts. Persistence and determination alone are omnipotent. The slogan "press on" has solved and will always solve the problems of the human race."

—Calvin Coolidge

PS. *I would not go into my face-to-face interview without a 30-60-90-Day Plan. You can learn more about how to create a plan on my blog:*

30-60-90-Day Plan – How To Create and Use It to Knock Their Socks Off in the Job Interview

http://careerconfidential.com/30-60-90-day-plan-how-to-create-and-use-it-to-knock-their-socks-off-in-the-job-interview/

If You Liked This eBook, Please Give It 5 Stars!

Reader reviews are so important...both for the success of this book and for me, so I know that I have given you what you need to be wildly successful in your next phone interview.

If you now feel as if you can tackle your next phone interview with confidence, let me know!

If you put the tips and principles of this book into practice and it results in an amazing phone interview for you, let me know!

Review this book here:

http://www.amazon.com/How-Ace-Your-Phone-Interview-ebook/product-reviews/B00HIFREIG/

Additional Resource Guide

Free Apps for iPhone, iPad and Android

Job Interview Questions and Answers

Free interactive video app lets you **practice your answers** to tough interview questions with Peggy McKee in an easy-to-use mock interview format.

Learn more here:

   http://jobinterviewquestionsandanswersapp.com/

Resume Review Pro

Improve your resume in **less than 10 minute**s with the top 'must do' resume tips from Peggy McKee.

Learn more here: http://resumereviewproapp.com/

Job Search Tips

Stand out and get the job with this comprehensive app that gives you **a strong resume, attention-getting cover letters, and more interviews.**

Learn more here: http://jobsearchtipsapp.com/

Free Training Webinars

Career Confidential offers weekly online training sessions (webinars) to arm you with smart, insightful, cutting-edge tips and strategies for your **resume, job search, and interviews.**

** See current webinars and how to enroll here:

https://careerconfidential.com/training-webinars/

More eBooks by Peggy McKee on amazon.com

How to Answer Interview Questions

See description, reviews, and get the book here:

http://www.amazon.com/Answer-Interview-Questions-Peggy-McKee-ebook/dp/B00AQ4CAFI/ref=la_B007NIWBS6_1_1?s=books&ie=UTF8&qid=1387704474&sr=1-1

How Do You Prepare For an Interview?

See description, reviews, and get the book here:
http://www.amazon.com/How-Do-You-Prepare-Interview-ebook/dp/B00BBJW2XW/ref=la_B007NIWBS6_1_2?s=books&ie=UTF8&qid=1387704474&sr=1-2

Finding a Job Fast Using a 30 / 60 / 90 Day Plan

See description, reviews, and get the book here:
http://www.amazon.com/Finding-Job-Fast-Using-Plan-ebook/dp/B007N5I9A8/ref=la_B007NIWBS6_1_3?s=books&ie=UTF8&qid=1387704474&sr=1-3

Career Confidential Products

Career Confidential is your 'go-to' resource for tools and coaching that get you HIRED. We help job seekers worldwide get jobs fast.

Explore customizable, unique, and powerful tools for a wildly successful job search here:

https://careerconfidential.com/job-search-tools/

Career Confidential Blog

Get the latest articles and tips for your job search success!

https://careerconfidential.com/blog/

Made in the USA
Las Vegas, NV
11 November 2020